531971218322832 7 **SEVEN** 823825
171231335724525O 192373

Book design by Tim Murray, paperbackdesign.com/books
Text set primarily in Minion, by Robert Slimbach

Throne Publishing Group 2329 N Career Ave. #215
Sioux Falls, SD 57107

25319712183228327823825934232171231 3
525019231339422122191949183761861439
335130187882 92 # SEVEN 14
3998716619818181 16
2214879442502 7 91

A Proven System for Achieving Financial Affluence

DR. DOUGLAS SEA

THRONE
PUBLISHING GROUP

Contents

Our relationship
with money
permeates
all other
relationships.

INTRODUCTION

Where It All Begins:
3 Key Relationships

There is no secret to wealth, but there is a system—the 7 Accounts System.

It's a time-tested blueprint for growing wealth and achieving authentic affluence. No matter where you're at today, whether $10,000 in debt or $500,000, *Seven* is your path forward. The following pages contain the first steps toward financial independence, freedom from unanticipated tax burden, having time and money to enjoy incredible experiences with your family, and much more.

What surprises people most is where this system begins. It doesn't start with your wallet; it starts with you and your three key relationships. These are the fundamental relationships we have with ourselves, with others, and with money.

RELATIONSHIP WITH SELF

Generally, we focus on the end results before anything else. We get tunnel vision and see only the ultimate goal we're trying to achieve. But guess what comes before results? The inputs. After all, our yield stems directly from what we sow.

When it comes to defining your three key relationships, what are your thoughts? What you think about matters. What's in your mind manifests in your actions, and how you act shapes your chances.

Frank Outlaw phrased it well when he wrote "Watch your thoughts, for they become your words. Watch your words, for they become your actions. Watch your actions, for they become your habits. Watch your habits, for they become your character."

So financial transformation begins first with mental remodeling. Think of it like a software upgrade for approaching life, work, and money. This upgrade changes everything by reorienting us to what matters most, the three key relationships that govern and guide us all. At first glimpse, these connections seem self-evident. But let's take a closer look.

Imagine you're enjoying yourself at a party. You mingle with friends, colleagues, acquaintances—and inevitably—you make new connections as well. Now, what's the classic first line in every initial conversation?

"What do you do?"

Nine times out of ten, this is the first question we

ask one another. Why is that? Why do we start with our careers as the jumping-off point for new relationships?

It's because we seek to define and interact with others the same way we do with ourselves.

You see, the first way we view ourselves is often governed by external labels—who we are and what we do. We're chiropractors, teachers, financial advisors, retail managers, consultants. We're fathers, mothers, brothers, and sisters. Our identities are first defined as relative to other people, but say nothing about how we relate to ourselves.

Our internal relationship has played second fiddle for so long. As a result, this is a new concept to many of us. Our identities become the sum total of what we can achieve relative to others, instead of who we are regardless of our success. While the people in both our lives and our careers certainly shape us, they're not the definition of who we are.

Our belief system, however, is such a force.

Your internal dialogue and the unique facets of your own personality are what define you. These are the forum in which we meet with ourselves and ultimately find the will, the power, and the purpose to grow.

When we define ourselves wholly by our profession or the people around us, we sacrifice our identities. This is one of the most purposeful forces at our disposal. If we know who we are and what we value, we set the course for our lives rather than allowing someone else to do it for us.

What is your self-talk? Are you negative and harsh with yourself? Or maybe you let yourself off the hook and constantly make excuses for a sloppy work ethic? You always award yourself a participation trophy.

Think about it like this. You speak to yourself according to how you view yourself. The way you view yourself determines how you view and interact with others. After all, we bring ourselves into all of our interactions with other people. If you find yourself consistently struggling in your relationships, the problem may be with you. You may be the only common denominator. Remember that wherever you go, there you are.

RELATIONSHIPS WITH OTHERS

The hierarchy of what and who is most important to you will jump to the forefront of any conversation. Your default behavior may be to control and domineer others. In other words, if you behave like an arrogant jerk, that will shine through pretty quickly.

Alternatively, if you're kind, inviting, and self-possessed, you are likely operating from a much healthier internal ecosystem. And therein lies the principle: the healthier your relationship with yourself, the healthier it will be with others.

This is because we bring every part of ourselves into all of our relationships. The good, the bad, and the ugly. But it's very difficult to change —perhaps even impossible— if we don't first understand where our behavior towards others comes from.

There is a third relationship in life that's equally as important as the first two.

RELATIONSHIP WITH MONEY

Our relationship with money influences and governs the connections we have to ourselves and with other people.

I recently had a telephone conversation with two young doctors who are husband and wife. She's worried they will be unable to keep their business open another week because their patient volume has plummeted. In fact, their staff is making more money than them.

It's no surprise this situation has created tremendous stress in both their professional and personal lives. Sadly, the wife threatened to leave her husband if the business fails and they cannot maintain their lifestyle. Even if their relationship was once strong, the inability to pay the bills has placed a terrible strain on their marriage.

There isn't some magic number that your family's income must reach to avoid a similar stress response. Sometimes, even if all of the liabilities are covered, being unable to buy a boat, remodel the kitchen, or fly first class still creates tension.

Financial psychologist Dr. Brad Kontz confirms in his book Wired for Wealth that money can indeed buy a modicum of happiness. His research suggests that, in the US, a family with a combined income of less than $50,000 per year will be less happy than those with a greater income. However, the defining line is $50,000 per year. Families with incomes of greater than $50,000 per year do not experience a greater happiness quotient. So while happiness may increase up to the point one's basic needs are met, it halts after that. Simply put, if money could buy happiness, there would be no unhappy rich people.

Our relationship with money permeates all other relationships. It's no wonder that disagreements over money are one of the leading causes of divorce.

Will turning this husband and wife's business around solve the relationship problems between them? I don't know, but I do know that if the business doesn't improve, the relationship will not improve either.

Long ago, people worried only about the most basic needs. We hunted, gathered, and grew our own food. We built shelters and fetched water from wherever it could be found. And if these basic survival needs were not met, the family unit suffered or ceased to exist entirely.

Thousands of years later, our basic survival needs are still with us. The game has simply changed in how we keep score. It's not enough to have provision, we must also have and display affluence. We relate to money on this level because we relate to others this way.

If we define our identities relative to our achievements and other people, we are in direct competition with them. So to feel good about ourselves, we need to be winners. And guess what winning means in our culture? The one with the most toys and the highest net worth wins.

We can view these three key relationships like a three-legged stool. Each leg supports the others. If you take away one of the legs, the stool topples and loses functionality. We need to have a system in place to recognize and remedy the weaknesses with our own relational stools.

Years ago, I heard Zig Ziglar tell a story about a pot roast that illustrates the perspective shift many of us need. The Ziglars were preparing for Christmas dinner when he noticed his sister cutting the end off the roast before putting it in the pan to cook. He asked her why she did this.

She replied, "That's the way mom always made it. Why don't we go ask her?"

So they did. And their mother replied, "That's the way grandma made it. Why don't we go ask her?"

So they asked their grandma. She replied, "That's the only way the pot roast would fit in my pan!"

For three generations, the Ziglars cut off the end of the pot roast and nobody knew why. How many things in your life could you be unaware of? What untrue thoughts govern your self-talk? What harmful habits do you carry with you into relationships? Where are you continually going wrong with your money?

Financially speaking, what pot roast do you keep cutting short without knowing why?

Lifestyle creep is like ivy. It grows year after year, making an almost imperceptible climb.

CHAPTER 1
Lifestyle Creep

The key to acquiring affluence is simply to spend less than you produce. Invest the difference and don't lose the principle. Nobody likes to hear that. It's not flashy. It's not fun. But financial guidance that doesn't start there is as good as counting on winning the lottery for your retirement plan.

Here's the truth. You simply cannot get rich by spending more money than you make. Period. It's like digging a hole and expecting to end up standing on the summit of Mt. Everest—you're going in the wrong direction!

Gravity works the same no matter where you live, whether you're in Hong Kong or San Francisco. If you drop a brick, it's going to fall. It's a universal law.

The key to wealth is the same. If you consistently spend less than you produce, you will always be able to grow your principle.

If you can start counting on that like you count on gravity, then get ready for your life to change. If you embrace this truth and have the discipline to stick with it, then the 7 Accounts System will work for you every time. Discipline begins with identifying the most common financial ailment in America: lifestyle creep.

Lifestyle creep is like ivy. It grows year after year, making an almost imperceptible climb. Then, before you know it, it's crawled up your siding and into the gutters. Lifestyle creep is the steady rise of your cost of living against your income. This is a direct result of how our tastes and expectations change as we grow older.

I grew up in a middle-class environment. My father was an educator and my mother stayed at home, with the exception of occasional substitute teaching. We never went to Disney World. We never vacationed in Europe or stayed in fancy hotels. Most of our traveling was around the neighborhood or day trips. When I went to college, my parents helped me where they could. But the financial responsibility was mostly mine to bear.

I recall going out for pizza with my buddies on Friday evenings. We would take turns snatching leftovers from the other customers' plates before the bus person cleaned their table. A free meal with enough pocket change left over for a cold beer. Talk about stretching a dollar!

Then I graduated. The years passed by and I steadily earned more income. But do you think my tastes have remained static? Not even close. They've evolved and grown in proportion to my income. In other words, I don't take my family out for a nice dinner only to send my kids foraging for appetizers from the crumbs left by other patrons. And my taste in adult beverages has evolved from beer by the pitcher to wine by the bottle.

But this happens to us all, right? Before you know it, you've moved into a new financial neighborhood where your income is within 20 percent of your neighbors' salary. For example, if you live in a gated community, it may be standard practice to own a car that "speaks" a foreign language and send your kids to a private school.

Is there a certain brand of tennis shoe that your kids refuse to wear? Have you graduated from JC Penney to shop exclusively at Nordstrom? Can Formica countertops still suffice or will only hard surfaces do?

Now, don't misunderstand me. There is nothing wrong with having nice things as long as you can still pay down your debts, save for the future, and give to charity. The problem is when you've reached the point that your tastes exceed your income. That's when lifestyle creep has set in.

This is the mistake most people make. As their business grows and develops, so does their spending. If their revenue increases by $2,000 per month, then their spending ticks up by that much or even more. This cycle then continues to repeat itself. This is how people who earn seven figures or more are still buried in debt.

Whether you're a millionaire or making minimum wage, you'll always be moving backwards if you spend more than you make. This is lifestyle creep. To beat it, remember the AWA Formula: awareness, willingness, and ability.

The very first step in solving any problem is to first acknowledge the problem exists. Become aware. Think about it this way. If you're unaware that you're spending the same amount of money or more than you earn, then you're unaware that your lifestyle is creeping out of control. Wealth or affluence is created by earning more money than you spend and investing or saving the difference.

It really is that simple.

If you are a high-income earner yet spend everything you make, you will never be wealthy. You may have an enviable lifestyle, but you will never be rich. Faster than anything else, lifestyle creep will sabotage your ability to gain financial independence and achieve your desired level of affluence. You must be aware of this hidden enemy to your wealth-building efforts and guard against it.

Not long ago, I had a client that was relatively new in practice. As we reviewed her practice and were studying the business' overhead, I discovered she was spending 8% of her current annual income on magazine subscriptions for her office. I advised that if she didn't control her overhead costs, she'd soon be out of practice. After all, she didn't even realize that she was spending $6,000 per year on periodicals.

But do you see what her first problem was? It wasn't that she was misallocating funds. She was unaware of how she was allocating them. The primary issue was she had no idea where her money was actually going.

This is where AWA comes into play. You must first be aware of how you're spending money to correct the course of your budget. If you find yourself in a financial hole, your first question must be "Where is all my money going?"

From there, take a clear and honest look at your finances. Even if it hurts, you must move from an awareness of where your money is going to a willingness to put an end to misuse.

I've discovered many things after years of advising clients regarding their personal relationship with money. One of the most difficult things for people is to reduce their perceived standard of living. In short, cutbacks are emotionally taxing and very painful. Once lifestyle creep has set in, it's very difficult to trim it back.

Consider this approach. Unless you have a looming financial crisis pending that requires a major pivot (bankruptcy, foreclosure, divorce etc.), commit to maintaining your current lifestyle and then grow your business. Put your shovel down, stop digging, and eliminate your lifestyle creep.

For example, let's say you get an unexpected $5,000 bonus or your practice nets an extra $2,000 this month.

Don't spend it! This is where the ability of AWA formula steps in. If your income increases but your expenditures stay the same, you will begin to build wealth.

You'll learn more about this when the entire 7 Accounts System is presented in subsequent chapters. Maintaining your current standard of living is a major tenant of this book. By halting lifestyle creep, you can lessen your financial obligations while preserving your current lifestyle. Stop allowing your lifestyle to continually expand. Take the money that's leftover each month and start knocking down your debt, saving, or even have some fun with it.

CHAPTER QUESTIONS

1. Has lifestyle creep made its way into your life?

2. Where are the top three areas this has happened?

3. How will you address it?

When you find a system that works every time—like this one—you've found guaranteed success.

CHAPTER 2
The Nine Rules Of Affluence

Americans are fond of statements like "Rules were made to be broken". And while that might look good on a poster, that advice will certainly break something if taken seriously. But it won't be the rules of affluence laid out in this chapter. It will be your bank account!

The nine rules of affluence are the paving stones for the 7 Accounts System. Each principle builds upon the other and forms an extraordinarily solid foundation.

THE NINE RULES ARE:

1. Spend everything you earn
2. Spend every dollar once
3. Never mingle your money
4. Savings is a habit

   5. It is difficult (if not impossible) to accumulate wealth while in debt

   6. Planned consumption

   7. No debt-reduction stress

   8. Strive to maintain your current lifestyle

   9. If you can't pay cash, you can't afford it

RULE 1: SPEND EVERYTHING YOU EARN

"Wait a second," you might be thinking. "Doesn't that seem a little counterintuitive?" Indeed it does! Why would I be advising you to spend all your money when the purpose of this system is to eliminate debt and enhance prosperity by consuming less than you earn?

The answer lies in human nature.

Culturally we have become encouraged us to spend or consume everything we make. The predictable result is that saving is at an all-time low. Even those with strong financial training have adopted a more cavalier attitude toward debt. Credit cards and ever-increasing spending proclaim "Live for today! Tomorrow will take care of tomorrow."

Instead of trying to convince you to go against a cultural norm, go ahead spend every penny you make. There is a catch. You only get to spend that money by depositing it into one of the accounts in the 7 Accounts System. Once the money has been spent into one of your accounts, it is no longer yours. It now belongs to that specified account and is only to be used for its designated purpose. We'll begin discussing the system in detail in the next chapter. But for now, just know that each week your income will be "spent" into one of your seven accounts for later distribution.

RULE 2: SPEND EVERY DOLLAR ONCE

If you follow Rule #1 and spend everything you earn, you will automatically follow Rule #2, spending every dollar once. Appreciating this rule and spending all of your income every week into one of your Named Accounts gives your money a job and a purpose. For example, dollars spent weekly into the tax account are no longer available for paying off your credit cards, buying groceries or used for investing. This income has been spent. Building affluence is more emotional than logical. Making incremental deposits into your accounts lessens the emotion involved with paying your financial obligations.

RULE 3: NEVER MINGLE YOUR MONEY

The reason I named this financial system the "7 Accounts System" is pretty obvious—there are seven accounts. Each of them has a designated purpose and represents the key areas most families will need to address financially. There are seven separate accounts for a reason. It is very important for you to use each account for its intended purpose and never mingle your money. If you keep all of your money together and maintain one larger account balance, you will easily deceive yourself into thinking you are wealthier than you are. That illusion will vanish once you have to write a large check from your prime account. Creating affluence is more emotional and behavioral than tactical.

This rule is short and sweet but is paramount to the system's success. Once your money has been "spent" into one of your accounts, it's gone and cannot be moved from one account to another. Your money never mingles.

RULE 4: SAVINGS IS A HABIT

At its essence, a habit is any behavior you perform on autopilot without having to force yourself to do it.

Habits are built through repetition and every habit results in an outcome, whether good or bad. Let's say, for example, your desired outcome is to run a marathon. If you haven't run since high school, you're not going to hit the pavement and jog 26.2 miles straight away. Rather, you're going to start with a half-mile. Then one mile. Then two and so on. Little by little, you'll build endurance for the race you'd like to run.

Physically, we all get this. It's not difficult to grasp. However, when it comes to money, we're shocked that we can't jump straight into an ideal rhythm. It takes time to start saving a solid percentage of our income every month.

Just like running a marathon, the habit of saving needs to be built little by little. The key to creating the habit is to save weekly without exception.

I've seen it time and again. If you aim for monthly savings, you'll run out of money before you run out of month.

I haven't missed a single weekly deposit in 27 years. Not even when I broke the transverse process on one of my vertebrae! Seriously, even if you fracture your spine, get to the bank and deposit your savings. It's that important.

When you are starting a new savings habit, keep in mind that the amounts don't matter just yet. What matters is consistency. Focus on saving money every single week rather than aiming for a lofty amount.

In fact, when I first started in practice, I was only able to save between ten and twenty dollars a week. This was hardly the mark of wealth and prosperity I'd envisioned when I became a doctor. But it was instrumental in building my saving habit. It was embarrassing at times to walk into a bank and deposit such a small amount. But I did it.

With those ten dollar deposits, a seed was planted and began to grow. Every mighty oak begins as an acorn.

RULE 5: IT IS DIFFICULT (IF NOT IMPOSSIBLE) TO ACCUMULATE WEALTH WHILE IN DEBT

If you want to get yourself out of a hole, the first thing you need to do is stop digging. So if you want to get out of debt, step one is to quit borrowing. Never borrow again? Seems counterintuitive again, doesn't it?

But consider this. Even if you took out a mortgage yesterday, you will be debt-free in thirty years if you don't borrow another penny! That itself is something to celebrate! The typical American believes debt is a normal part of life. I have never seen a consumer debt without a payoff date. No debt with the exception of our national debt is perpetual. The problem is the consumer continues to add to the balance and the debt appears to be perpetual.

Most people simply go from one 30-year mortgage to the next. They live in their first home for five to seven years when their house payments are mostly interest. Then it's time to upgrade to a newer house. So the starter home is placed on the market and the owner pays a seven percent commission to the real estate agent. Then they go pick up some more furniture to fill the extra rooms in their new home.

But do they pick up where they left off and get a 23-year mortgage? Hardly. Instead, they get a brand new 30-year loan with a fatter monthly payment as well. Seven years later, the cycle typically repeats itself again!

Let's imagine for a minute that your entire debt load (including your mortgage, business loans, cars, student loans, and credit cards) is $500,000.

If you are paying an average of eight percent interest, that is $40,000 a year in interest alone. Your business has to produce around $100,000 a year (assuming 30 percent in taxes and 40 percent in overhead costs) just to cover the interest on your debts. So if you do the math, you'll see why it is so difficult to accumulate wealth while you are in debt.

To jumpstart your financial recovery, you may need a little "financial triage." If you can't discipline your credit card use, you may need some "plastic surgery". And that means cutting up those credit cards. You also might need to unload some financial baggage by selling the things you simply don't need.

Will it be unpleasant? Probably. But in the interest of becoming debt-free, consider selling extra vehicles, your boat, jet skis, or even your vacation property.

My advice is if you can't pay off an item within twenty four months, sell it. If you want to move ahead, you must release yourself from the weights that keep pulling you backward.

RULE 6: PLANNED CONSUMPTION

Impatience leads to debt because it prods you to take shortcuts. Sign for the loan. Swipe the card. Borrow money from your future to satisfy today's desires.

But the principle of planned consumption dictates that you only purchase something when you have the money in hand. And you can't steal from another one of your seven accounts!

If you or your family want something that's not allocated for in one of your accounts, you must plan and save for it prior to making the purchase. This habit alone pays dividends. Often, when someone is practicing this principle for the first time, they commit to saving for a new luxury car.

Once they've saved the required $50,000, many decide that the new car smell just isn't worth all that sacrifice and work. So they buy a slightly used car and a big chunk of that $50,000 is still in the bank. They have a great car and a head start on the next nice thing they want.

A collateral benefit to this principle is when we plan to consume, we are by default planning to save as well. When we earmark dollars for specific destinations, we prevent them from being misspent. In effect, you'll never spend a dollar that you were supposed to have saved, invested, or paid to a vendor.

Planned consumption is both a plan to spend and to save. It works in tandem with principle three, *Savings As A Habit*.

RULE 7: NO DEBT-REDUCTION STRESS

My wife and I experienced acute debt-reduction stress years ago when we committed ourselves to becoming debt-free. We consumed ourselves with that goal and saved and scrimped every spare penny, nickel, and dime to accomplish it.

Twenty-four months later, we were completely debt free—house and everything. But we also had no assets. So in effect, we were zeroed out. We also experienced little fun and only gave a pittance in those twenty-four months. Our lives were pretty unbalanced.

That is why, in retrospect, the 7 Accounts System is now designed to incorporate consistent debt reduction, savings, fun, and giving. It's not just about eliminating debt. This plan reduces most of the stress encountered with drastic lifestyle changes like those we endured to get out of debt so quickly.

Looking back, we would have much rather been in debt an extra year or two rather than live through the crucible we put ourselves through. This is another reason why this system is so effective. It balances wonderful financial outcomes while being sustainable, fun, and relationally healthy.

RULE 8: STRIVE TO MAINTAIN YOUR CURRENT LIFESTYLE

As we discovered in the previous chapter, it's very easy for lifestyle creep to set in. What's not so easy, however, is trimming the fat from today's standard of living. Going backward is extremely difficult. What we once considered a luxury we now consider a necessity.

A quick way to knock out debt and accumulate a lot of savings is to sell your house. Pay off your debt with the equity and move into a more economical space. But again, you invite serious debt-reduction stress.

Rather than focus on aggressive debt reduction and monastic living, make it a point to stop lifestyle creep dead in its tracks. As your business grows, maintain your current lifestyle and expenditures. If you keep your standard of living static, you will be able to save your increased profits and accelerate your accumulation of wealth.

RULE 9: IF YOU CAN'T PAY CASH, YOU CAN'T AFFORD IT

This rule sounds so simple. And in principle, it is. But it requires discipline, conviction, and patience. This rule is the key to maintaining your current standard of living.

So make the first step easy on yourself. Cut the plastic cord! If you stop buying on credit, you'll never spend more than you earn.

Debt is the ability to pretend. It's the way millions of people lie to themselves and to their neighbors. Debt simply allows us to temporarily act and live as if we've earned more than we actually have.

When misused, credit cards are devices to indulge pretentiousness. They entice you to live beyond your means, often in an attempt to impress others or comfort yourself.

However, it's important to maintain perspective at the same time. Credit cards are just tools. A tool used correctly can be an effective way to enhance your business. After all, you don't blame the baseball for a broken window. You blame the kid who threw it.

It's nearly impossible to book a flight or hotel room without a credit card. Inappropriate credit card usage invites financial hardship and even bankruptcy.

These rules, when used in concert with the 7 Accounts System, will help you expand your business, eliminate your debt, and create financial prosperity for your family without fail.

Your first task is to incorporate these rules into your thoughts and let them shape your view of money. Write them down and keep them in your wallet or checkbook.

Jot them on sticky notes and put them on your mirror. Do whatever you must to keep them in front of you every day. Remember, habits are built through repetition so find ways to rehearse these rules so they can become part of you and your family's DNA.

One of the misunderstood secrets to rules, truths, and principles is that they're not constrictive. They're liberating. These nine principles aren't meant to inhibit your lifestyle. They're not a cage placed on your happiness or enjoyment. Rather, each is a rung to the life you've always wanted. When you find a system that works every time— like this one—you've found guaranteed success.

However, just like a ladder, you must faithfully climb each rung if you're ever going to reach the top. The disciplined climb is the consistent one. If you faithfully implement these principles in your life, you will see a positive financial impact. And when it comes time to objectively measure your progress, simply look at the numbers.

People often lie to one another and even to themselves. But numbers never lie!

CHAPTER QUESTIONS

1. Which rule stuck out to you the most?

2. How can you apply it immediately?

3. How do you expect your life will change if you implement each principle?

The affluence
gap is the space
between your
earnings and
what you spend.

CHAPTER 3
The 7 Accounts System

The 7 Accounts System allows you to build the financial future you've always wanted.

You can predictably create a lifestyle that allows you to pay cash for purchases, stay current on taxes, pay down debt, create wealth, donate to worthy causes and, of course, have some fun along the way.

When I struck out and started my own practice I knew that I wasn't all that smart. But knowing that is what made me smart. I didn't have all the answers so I sought wisdom wherever I could find it. I never intended to create a financial management system. Instead, the 7 Accounts System was simply the culmination of how I led my life and career from inception until today.

In reality, the system was more of an accidental discovery than a deliberate creation. It evolved over many years and was fine tuned over time.

I can't claim any brilliance on my part But I can tell you with confidence that the 7 Accounts System will enable financial independence, freedom from debt, and allow the creation of a secondary income source from your accumulated investment portfolio. The goal is to live a creative lifestyle and do the things we were placed on this earth to do. It's about putting in the intense, short-term work and creating significant, long-term gain.

In fact, it was only quantified when a business partner asked me to teach him my financial system.

I said, "What financial system?"

He replied, "You know. That thing you do with all those different accounts. You need to teach your financial system to our clients."

I first taught the 7 Accounts System about twenty years ago and the success stories from our clients have been pretty amazing.

One doctor sent me a picture of a giant check with his picture on it. The check's amount was what he paid to the IRS! This was huge for him because he previously hated paying taxes and it was always a stressful time. But by utilizing the system, he saved his tax money every year and there is no associated strain paying the IRS. In fact, he now knows that the more he pays them, the better off he is as well. Talk about a different take on tax season!

In addition to seeing my clients get a new outlook

on taxes, I also have a front row seat to how transformative getting out of debt is. It's a happy day when that last mortgage coupon payment is made and the "debt shackles" clang to the floor.

Cars, trips, family time, vacations, and swimming with dolphins are some of the most enriching stories I hear from our clients, just to name a few. Not to mention the overwhelming sense of liberation from the true bondage debt brings. These stories could become your story by applying the 7 Accounts System to your life and the proper utilization of the Fun Account. They're using that money to have bigger and better experiences with their families, go on nicer vacations and order from restaurant menus without looking at the price first.

They take extended trips with their entire family without any debt to worry about and with no need for credit cards. They plan for what they want and can live in the moment without worrying about paying for a trip six months down the road. And because of the 7 Accounts System, this has simply become their lifestyle.

I am not promising this will be easy. There will certainly be discomfort in the process. However, if you consistently follow the system over a period of time, you will dig yourself out of debt. The more you make and the less you spend, the bigger shovel you will have. You can get out of debt and start achieving a sense of affluence you may never have thought possible before.

Here's my promise: it will be worth it.

The affluence gap is the space between your earnings and what you spend. For many that number is a negative, which means they're spending more than they're earning. Regardless of your total income, if you spend it all, there will be nothing left to accelerate debt payments, invest, give, or enjoy. So bridging this gap may require you to decrease your discretionary spending, increase your income by investing in your business or coaching, or maybe even both.

Chances are if you're reading this book you have enough income that you're very near bridging the affluence gap. Your practice or business may be surviving yet not quite thriving. By applying the principles that follow, your income gap will narrow quickly and the bridge to an affluence you may have never imagined will appear. Follow the principles outlined in this book, live on less than you make, invest the difference and stay consistent. You won't have to win the lottery to live in abundance!

Now, what is the 7 Accounts System?

As the name indicates, the 7 Accounts System utilizes seven different accounts, preferably in seven different banks, as "holding tanks" or temporary accounts.

Weekly deposits are made into each account until sufficient amounts have been accumulated to trigger the appropriate action. The reason the accounts are separate is to completely deter any "mingling" of funds. The moment you start to cross-pollinate accounts, you've gone off course and have broken away from the system. In fact, this is such a crucial point that I recommend each of your seven accounts be held by seven different banks. This adds a layer of difficulty to transferring money from one "tank" to another.

Additionally, one of the major benefits of working the 7 Accounts System is its contribution in attracting new clients. Take a guess at one of the largest occupational categories of my practice. Banking professionals. Remember, people buy what is familiar to them. Frequenting seven banks every week makes you familiar to a significant number of potential customers. All at no cost to you.

Account Overview:

ACCOUNT ONE IS YOUR "BUSINESS OVERHEAD".
This account is simply your existing business checking account. This serves three purposes:
1. A holding tank for business revenue.
2. A payment method for all business/practice bills.
3. Fund distribution to the remaining six accounts.

ACCOUNT TWO IS YOUR "TAX ACCOUNT".
This is a checking or cash management account because you have to be in a position to write your quarterly tax payments. You don't need full check-writing privileges here because you're only going to write four or five checks out of this account each year.

ACCOUNT THREE IS YOUR "HOUSE ACCOUNT" OR "PERSONAL EXPENDITURE ACCOUNT".

Whatever it takes to run your household is allocated here. Every household I know of already has this checking account established.

ACCOUNT FOUR IS YOUR "DEBT-REDUCTION ACCOUNT".

This will likely be a savings or some kind of cash management account. Its purpose will be a holding tank until you have enough money in it to pay off one of your debts.

ACCOUNT FIVE IS YOUR "WEALTH ACCOUNT".

This is also a holding tank until you accumulate a large enough balance to trigger some sort of an investment activity. For some people, the trigger amount is anywhere from $500 to $10,000 or more. Simply save the funds in this account and then invest. Remember, any deposit into the Wealth Account is destined to be invested for the long term. These funds are not to be consumed for a perceived short term need.

ACCOUNT SIX IS YOUR "GIVING ACCOUNT".

This is a simple checking account intended to hold funds with which to bless others. The recipients could be your church, the food bank, or your friends or relatives in need.

ACCOUNT SEVEN IS YOUR "FUN ACCOUNT".
This account is the debt-reduction stress relief valve. It's a good place to keep spending money for mountain bikes, golf clubs, or Gucci shoes. This is the money you get to spend more frivolously so have fun with it!

Let's take a close-up of each account and find out how establishing and maintaining each one will bring you closer to your wealth-building goals!

CHAPTER QUESTIONS
1. Which account is most surprising to you?

2. Which account will be the most difficult for you?

3. How do you expect your life will change when you implement this system?

At the end of the day, what matters is how much you keep, not how much you make.

CHAPTER 4

Business Overhead Account

The first account in the 7 Accounts System is the Business Overhead Account. It's your existing business checkbook. All of your business' income is deposited into this account. To keep it simple, go with a business checking account here. These differ from personal accounts as they carry options that may help you as a business owner.

From this account, all business expenses are paid. The difference between the amount collected and checks written is your gross profit. This should be taken as a draw, salary, or as a dividend.

Over the years, I've analyzed hundreds of businesses and have seen overhead range from eighteen to eighty percent or more. Some new or struggling businesses were stuck with an overhead of over 100 percent!

However, your ratio of overhead to income never has to be a mystery. Here's a simple formula for determining that ratio:

1. Take the revenue figures from each of the preceding three months.
2. Calculate the monthly revenue average.
3. Average monthly expenditures over the same prior three-month timeframe.
4. Divide the average overhead by the average revenue.

Even if the figure returned shocks you, this isn't the time to bury your head in the sand like an ostrich. This is crucial information if you're going to advance your practice, business, and household.

Next, find what percentage of your overhead goes to expenses like labor, utilities, office supplies, etc. These numbers may also come as a surprise. Remember the doctor I mentioned earlier whose office spent eight percent of their overhead on magazines for the waiting room? She had no idea that she was spending so much.

Lowering your business overhead percentage requires increasing your income, decreasing your expenses, or both.

Is a monthly overhead of $15,000 too high? Well, it depends. That level of overhead would be considered very high at seventy five percent if the business is earning $20,000 a month. But if the business collects

$60,000 each month, that same overhead is only twenty five percent. In today's competitive marketplace, we like to see our clients shoot for a forty to fifty percent overhead range. This allows for greater profitability and growth potential.

Business owners must be realistic in their spending. Just because it's deductible doesn't mean it is a worthwhile expenditure. Even at the top marginal tax brackets, you still have to spend a dollar to save thirty nine cents in taxes.

Whatever the current overhead percentage of your office today, it's helpful to think of your business purchases as an investment. When you treat expenses as investments, your views will shift.

If you have been in practice for more than six months, you know how critical it is for your business to maintain and achieve viability. This is the point where more money is coming in than going out every month. Undercapitalization is the number one reason most businesses initially fail. A startup requires enough capital to sustain operations long enough to bridge the gap of expenses exceeding income.

Often, it can take six to twelve months for a startup practice to achieve viability. In addition to time, there are many other variables. An individual doctor's energy and willingness to meet new people, the office location, and the practice's operational systems are all important factors.

While going into debt is rarely a viable long-term wealth building strategy, there are occasions where it may be necessary. Unless you had the proverbial "rich uncle" to enhance your operation, you need some financed capital to get your business up and running. However, it's important to note that the decision to start with debt versus staying in debt are different matters entirely. Once you've achieved minimum viability, follow the 7 Accounts System and you will be able to maintain a healthy relationship with your income and a respect for your money.

Ultimately, your Business Overhead Account is there to help grow your business. So as you begin to look at all expenditures as investments, consider reinvesting in yourself as well. Are you going to reinvest a percentage of your revenue into growing the business? Will you invest in coaching, seminars, marketing, business development activities, or conferences?

Another aspect of reinvesting in your business is the equipment you're using. For me, my tables and chiropractic equipment had to be top of the line. Portable tables may be a practical purchase to reduce startup costs. But they are simply inappropriate in an office that has been established for over a year. It sends the wrong message to your patients, it screams that you are temporary.

Now, those are just a few of the many considerations that go into a tightly-budgeted "Business Overhead Account". But the point here is that you need to be the one managing this account. Don't let it manage you. Yes, control your expenses but keep an "investment mindset" when assessing your operations as well.

At the end of the day, it doesn't matter how much you make. What matters is how much you keep. This is the secret to bridging the affluence gap. Produce a good income, live below your means (both personally and professionally), and invest the difference.

CHAPTER QUESTIONS

1. What is your overhead to income ratio?

2. Is this surprising to you?

3. Where can you cut back to lower this number?

If you follow the system, there are no surprises. Just celebrations.

CHAPTER 5
Tax Account

As a chiropractic coach and business mentor for over twenty years, I have counseled doctors on a variety of issues. But one of the most difficult areas to gain traction with is tax trouble. Here, an ounce of prevention is certainly better than a pound of cure.

In my experience, the IRS makes a very poor business partner. If tax issues are looming, that must be your number one priority. I have seen too many doctors work hard, do well, fail to plan, and end up in what I refer to as "tax jail." They aren't physically in prison, but the level of bondage they experience is just as palpable as if they were incarcerated. If nothing else, their drive to succeed is locked up.

Taxes are typically paid quarterly so the payments can be quite large. I have paid my fair share of large tax checks and believe me, this can be a painful thing to do. If you're either short on money or emotionally unprepared, this experience can be devastating. I found the secret is to keep your funds dedicated to tax payments in a separate "Tax Account". Just like the rest, the only money that enters or leaves this account is either saved up for estimated taxes or used to discharge your tax liability.

If you keep your tax money mingled with the rest of your funds, it will be a very painful experience come the fifteenth of April. Especially so if you find you don't have the padding you thought you did. Or worse yet, you're overdrawn!

In my second year of business, I hired an accountant whom I thought was pretty sharp. In fact, he prepared and sent me a fourteen-page profit and loss disbursement journal every month. The figures on the page all looked like Greek to me. But I figured that the accountant had it all under control because we paid the man a lot of money for his guidance and expertise. At this early stage of my career, I had no clue as to how to interpret a profit and loss statement. I had a rudimentary appreciation of business though. I knew that if I profited, there was would be an income tax consequence. I had a rough idea what the marginal rate would be. So every week after paying my expenses (gross revenue, minus expenses, equals profit), I multiplied my marginal tax rate by the profit and made a deposit into my newly opened "Tax Account".

Thus, the second account of the 7 Accounts System was born. And it served us better than our suit-and-tie accountant.

April 15th rolled around and we visited with our accountant. He opened with the old "I've got good news and bad news" line. Ever the optimist, I asked for the good news first. He said the good news was we were very profitable last year. But the bad news was we were under withheld by $53,268!

Fortunately, I had diligently minded my Tax Account and made the appropriate deposits each week. In fact, I'd actually banked $56,000 in my tax account. Our taxes were paid on time and I still had money left over. My wife and I signed our returns, wrote the largest check of our lives, fired the fancy accountant, and went out for dinner to celebrate. We got a tax refund!

I was so grateful that I didn't take the $53K and buy a sports car! Had I squandered that money and not saved it, I would have definitely been in tax jail. It's amazing how unemotional this event was and how it established many of the 7 Accounts System rules and philosophies.

The secret was making the weekly deposits. Once the funds were deposited into a specific account, the money was already spent on an emotional level. So the separation had already been happening in smaller manageable doses. That's why there are no tears when tax time rolls around. You can allocate the money without emotion.

If your business does need an accountant for more

than filing annual paperwork, don't settle for a nice office or expensive business cards. As with all people you trust to help your business, they need to be interviewed. Do they appreciate your philosophy as a business owner? Will they respect your wishes? And in my case, did he enjoy the fine art of communicating with his clientele?

The principle to glean here is this: it's your money. Do not abdicate control of it to anyone.

The key to a healthy Tax Account is to plan the expenditure. Technically, you may only pay taxes annually or quarterly. But the secret is contributing to your Tax Account every week. Ask your accountant your top marginal tax rate. Each week, put that percentage of your earnings into the Tax Account. Simple, easy, and stress-free. It is way easier to write a $500 check every week than it is to write a $26,000 check on tax day.

Remember though, tax laws change every year. If your business is growing, your tax rate may go up. So stay in communication with your accountant so that you're not working from old numbers and end up shocked by a significant tax liability. Tax problems will do more to derail your affluence path faster than anything. So pay attention and do the work one week at a time.

As you move forward with this system, things will begin to unlock for you financially. So you must understand that you will write some of the biggest checks of your life to the IRS in the years ahead. But you know what? That's okay. In fact, I want you in the highest tax bracket because that means your earnings are up. The larger the bill due to Uncle Sam, the better year you had! And I can say this with certainty. If you follow the system, there are no surprises. Just celebrations.

Top Marginal Ordinary and Capital Gains Tax Rates, 1913–2012

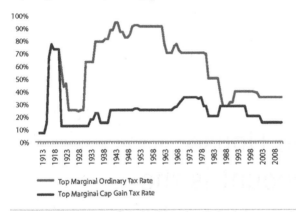

Source: Tax Policy Center, "U.S. Individual Income Tax: Personal Exemptions and Lowest and Highest Tax Bracket Tax Rates and Tax Base for Regular Tax, Tax Years 1913–2012," available at: taxpolicycenter.org/taxfacts /displayafact.cfm?DocID=543&Topic2id=30&Topic3id=39; CCH Incorporated, "2012 CCH Whole Ball of Tax," available at: cch.com/wbot2012/029CapitalGains.asp.

CHAPTER QUESTIONS

1. Do you have anxiety or uncertainty going into tax season?

2. Have you ever been surprised by a large tax bill?

3. How would your life change if you knew that your tax liability was completely covered?

The House Account is the first place where you can start bridging the affluence gap.

CHAPTER 6
House Account

The House Account is your personal checking account. From here, you'll pay personal expenses like your mortgage, utilities, groceries, and any other routine payments.

While this account may seem the most familiar and straightforward, there is a delicate balance that needs to be struck. You must allocate enough money to maintain your current standard of living, all while saving margin for debt reduction and investments.

This is also where you'll be tempted to either enable lifestyle creep or throw as much money at your debt as possible each month. But remember, neither path is realistic or sustainable over the long haul. And while there are some households in need of immediate "financial triage" to stem the bleeding, only do so after a serious review of your household's budget and needs.

At its crux, the House Account is the first place where you can start bridging the affluence gap. This is where you can begin earning more than you spend and investing the rest. This is your financial Great Divide. It's the watershed that divides the rigid accounts from the more flexible ones.

The first three accounts have very little—if any—discretionary status.

If you neglect to pay your office expenses, your doors won't stay open for long. Landlords and banks have a funny way of enforcing your obligation to them. If you don't pay your taxes, you really could end up in tax jail (and it's pretty tough to run a successful practice from there). And if you fail to keep your home financially solvent, the stress will erode your ability to produce and provide for your personal stakeholders.

The amount of money dedicated to this account is simply the weekly application of your monthly budget. Hopefully, you made a monthly budget earlier. If you haven't, do so now. Skip television this evening and invest the time in tallying up your monthly spending. Divide that figure by 4.3 (the average number of weeks in a month) and you have the magic number that you need to deposit into your House Account each week.

Visit www.sidecaredge.com/sidecar-services/seven to download the Budget Worksheet.

If your spouse works outside the home, my advice is to deposit his or her check directly into the House Account. Then your practice income can subsidize any shortfalls. That's the beauty of this approach. It frees up more funds to be reinvested into the business or to be funneled into the remaining four more discretionary accounts.

CHAPTER QUESTIONS

1. Does your standard of living tend to increase with your income?

2. What impact could an increased income reinvested into your business have?

3. What are some practical steps you can take to maintain your current lifestyle without increasing it?

Debt creates fear
which, over time,
leads to stress.

CHAPTER 7
Debt-reduction Account

Debt makes wealth accumulation exponentially more difficult.

Now, there are differing financial opinions regarding debt. Should you leverage it or leave it alone all together? I believe that it depends. Money problems and successes are more behavioral and emotional than they are tactical. Based on our empirical studies of many high-income earners, this opinion is verified daily.

Having zero debt is incredibly freeing for the small business owner. Unfortunately, I've consistently witnessed that businesses grow along with their personal budgets. In essence, they're simply earning more to spend more. But when all of their cash flow is passed through, no real headway has been made against debt. Their financial state is actually no better off than when they began.

Not only is that frustrating from my perspective, but it's continually disheartening for business owners.

Debt creates fear which, over time, leads to stress. Debt stress is a combination of both *how much* money you owe and *how many* creditors you owe. Envision owing $250,000 to sixteen different creditors ranging from car loans and credit cards to your mortgage. You have to write sixteen separate checks each month. If you get behind, you end up juggling payment schedules.

Now compare that to owing the exact same amount but your only creditor is your mortgage provider. Having only one check to write creates results in much less stress.

Hear me loud and clear on this. I'm not suggesting mortgaging your groceries or risking your home by opening a large home equity loan in order to consolidate your debt. This strategy rarely works. Those who attempt this without changing the underlying consumptive behavior are back full circle in short order. Only now they have a similar debt load in addition to a freshly minted home equity loan.

I simply want you to realize that each time you pay off a small debt, there is one less person with their hooks in you. You are one step closer to financial freedom.

So how should you go about starting a Debt-Reduction Account?

Step one is figuring out exactly how much debt you have.

Visit www.sidecaredge.com/sidecar-services/seven to
download the Debt List Worksheet.

First, take a debt inventory. Simply list all of your debts.
This includes car loans, back taxes, back child support,
mortgage, credits card(s), even the loan from your broth-
er- in-law. Every one counts. Now list all of these debts
from smallest to largest, regardless of interest rate.

That's right. Smallest to largest balance, not loan
interest or payoff dates.

Remember, we're trying to reshape your mindset
here. And to do this, you need some wins! Wouldn't you
love the extreme gratification of telling the credit card
company you don't want to have a relationship anymore?

By paying off the smallest debt first, you're reaching
another milestone as well.

First, you're eliminating one more entity that has
a claim on your wallet. Remember, debt stress is the
amount you owe *plus* the number of creditors you have.
By eliminating your first obligation, you are also freeing
up additional capital to accelerate all other debts.

Let's say you were paying $100 every month on
one credit card. Remember, you already have that
amount figured into your monthly budget. But now
that you've paid the card off, that $100 will continue to
be deposited every month from your House Account
your Debt-Reduction Account.

So now, you'll have that $100 plus the $285 already

going toward your car payment (your next smallest debt listed). That means you're now attacking your car loan at a rate of $385 per month. From here, continue to make the same payment every time you pay off a creditor. Just roll it up to the next largest debt.

Here's another strategy to consider. Continue to pay the scheduled payment (in this example the $285 per month) until you have accumulated enough in your Debt-Reduction Account to pay off the loan balance.

If you save $100 a week in your Debt-Reduction Account plus the additional $100 per month that was going to the credit card, you now have over $500 per month going to debt reduction. If you owe $5000 on your next smallest loan it would take you less than ten weeks to save enough to knock this debt out. If you add the paid off car loan and credit card to the additional $100 per week you are saving, your Debt-Reduction Account now yields almost $800 per month to pay off the next smallest debt. You can gain traction quickly through debt reduction.

Celebrate your small wins and reaffirm your commitment to getting out of debt completely. You'll soon experience a transformation in the way you look at this account. Rather than the red ink account, it becomes a prime gateway to bridging the affluence gap. You will reap both financial and emotional rewards if you discipline yourself to properly leverage and fund your Debt Reduction Account.

CHAPTER ACTION ITEMS

1. List your debts from smallest to largest.

2. List any monthly required payments next to each debt.

3. Calculate when you can have each paid off by working the Debt Reduction Account.

Getting rich is rarely an "event." It's a process that requires time, persistence, consistency, and, of course, money!

CHAPTER 8
Wealth Account

Once you've opened your personal Wealth Account, you will never be poor again. How could you be? You now have a wealth account. In fact, it will become impossible because you will continually accumulate and invest your wealth. This is the first step toward making your money work for you, instead of the other way around.

The Wealth Account works by serving as a trust to hold your weekly deposits until you've accumulated enough money to trigger investment events. Essentially, you will determine what increments you'd like to invest, be it every $5,000 or $10,000. Once your balance reaches this threshold, you invest it and start again.

There are two components to the Wealth Account. I call them Account 5A and Account 5B.

5A acts as a self-insurance fund. This is your rainy-day, *true* emergency money. It's the balance you'd have to fall back on if every bit of your income dried up in a day's time.

The balance you will hold in 5A contains three to six months living expenses. So, simply take the number you arrived at from compiling your monthly budget and multiply it by three, four, five, or six times—whatever number you feel comfortable with.

To begin, your first objective here is to get $1,000 deposited. When you're just beginning, this is your prime objective with your Wealth Account. In fact, this piece is so critical that I advise people to fund this account at the expense of all others. It gives you breathing room, reduces financial anxiety, and sparks a prosperity consciousness. Once you have the initial $1,000, however, proceed to funding the other seven accounts accordingly.

Now, let's assume that you've saved the first $1,000 emergency fund and are now transitioning into saving for six months of living expenses. As an example, we'll imagine that your family requires $5,000 per month to maintain the status quo. That means your 5A account should reach $30,000 before you stop allocating funds to it.

But once you've reached your target self-insurance policy, forget that you have it altogether! Resist the urge to dip in for Christmas gifts here or withdraw a bit for an impromptu vacation. This isn't simply a savings account— it's an *emergency* account.

It exists for when your car breaks down, your tooth cracks, someone gets sick, or any number of unfortunate situations life throws at you. To help you keep this account off-limits, don't worry about the interest rate. These funds should be invested in a CD or money market account. This needs to be an account that carries a penalty for accessing funds early. Wealth Account 5A is really an investment in your relationship with your spouse. Imagine the sparkle in your partner's eye after you have committed to providing financial security for the family, even in an a state of emergency.

Now that you understand 5A, let's move on to 5B. This will be the "holding tank" for your weekly deposits. The goal here is to define a target number to accumulate before triggering an investment event.

Let's say your target number is $5,000. This means that when 5B hits $5,000, you call your bond broker or investment counselor and move forward with an investment in that amount. It's as simple as that.

While this isn't exactly a book on investment advice, I do suggest remaining conservative with all investing activity until your family's finances have been secured.

I recommend beginning your financial plan with high-rated, tax-free municipal bonds. These type of bonds provide a guaranteed tax-free return. Consider investing your first $500,000-$1,000,000 this way. Then, your level of risk is up to your financial palette. However, make certain that your familial obligations are covered and met before you venture too far into high-risk territory.

Not losing your hard earned principle is one of the keys to saving large amounts of money. I have experienced it both ways: steady growth while producing more income to invest, and then never losing any of that income.

I've also learned the hard way. Here's where I'd encourage you to take a lesson from Ben Franklin. He wrote, "You have two ways to learn; from making your own mistakes or learning from mistakes other people have made. You can learn a tremendous amount from observing other people and the mistakes they have made."

If you can learn from others' mishaps, you don't have to make them yourself. Unfortunately, I've participated in some very wild and unpredictable schemes.

One year, a close friend, fellow chiropractor, and the godfather of one of my children approached me with an incredible opportunity. He'd happened into this opportunity about ten months earlier and since then, he'd enjoyed a consistent seven percent per month return.

Not too bad.

He'd done his due diligence. He made his deposits, received statements showing tens of thousands of return to his account. And he had even made several systematic cash calls and actually received his money back. So, after ten months of reassurance, he felt it was an opportunity to share with me. In fact, had he not and it continued to work, I would have been hurt that he didn't include me.

I met with his friend and immediately liked and

trusted him based on my experience and another friend's endorsement. So I decided to invest $100,000 with him. After two weeks, I received my first statement showing that I'd already earned a hefty $3,500!

My friend had been mentally spending this *lottery money* for almost a year and, lamentably, had taken psychic ownership of the huge appreciation in his account. It was working so well, in fact, he kept pumping more cash into it.

However, I soon noticed that communications with the so-called investor stopped completely. I stopped getting statements, received no return phone calls, and suddenly had no correspondence with the man I'd invested six figures.

I checked with my friend and he hadn't heard anything either. You can imagine the strain he began to feel.

By now you can see where this is headed. Our money was gone and so was he.

After some legal and political maneuvering, I discovered the US Treasury had become involved and this guy had relocated to a country without an extradition treaty. He had taken over $30 million with him!

Now I don't know about you, but I like sleeping well at night knowing my family's financial security is well provided. Learn from my mistake and remember, if an investment opportunity sounds too good to be true, it probably is.

Getting rich is rarely an "event." It's a process that requires time, persistence, consistency, and, of course, money!

One of the primary objectives of the 7 Accounts System is building the Wealth Account. It acts as your long term savings plan and can even be used as a retirement plan. The intended consequence a large Wealth Account balance is creating a secondary source of income. The interest produced by your Wealth Account begins to compound. This secondary source of income, if large enough, can replace the primary source of income you actively earn in your practice or job. If not sufficient to totally replace it, this passive income can subsidize your living needs. Just never touch the principle.

The benefit of a second income source provides you with an abundance of options. You have the ability to continue a fulfilling career or change careers altogether. You now have some serious options. You can go to work because you want to, not because you have to.

If you follow the 7 Accounts System, pay off all of your debt, and invest $1 million in tax-free municipal bonds that yield a five percent return, you will net $50,000 tax-free every year.

As your Wealth Account grows, so do the corresponding annualized returns. These returns are then re-invested into the Wealth Account. If you do not perform what I call "financial cannibalism"—that is, consuming your financial offspring by spending your interest—you will enjoy the beauty of compound interest. All the while, your money, net worth, and financial momentum will continue to grow exponentially.

Your consistent use of the Wealth Account through weekly deposits will do more to ensure your financial security and affluence than any other activity I know. As my practice grew and I became debt-free, I was able to save thousands of dollars a week because I had the habit and the system in place. Once the debt is eliminated, the growth of the Wealth Account is accelerated. The dollars that were once dedicated to build the Debt-Reduction Account are now funneled into the Wealth Account as you no longer have any debt. Remember the example of a $500,000 debt requiring $40,000 to address the interest obligation? With zero debt, all of those funds go to the Wealth Account. Without this system I am confident I would have been pondering the same question many of you ask.

"Hmm. I wonder where all my money went this year?"

CHAPTER QUESTIONS

1. What amount will your investment trigger points be?

2. How will you invest the funds?

3. What return can you expect?

Giving is not a
debt you owe, but
a seed you sow.

CHAPTER 9
Giving Account

Money is energy and energy has to flow. The Giving Account is set up to maintain our financial balance and keep the energy flowing throughout our lives. When we hoard our money, we become stagnant and stifled to the point where our ability to produce is harmed. But when we consistently give, the energy remains in a constant flow from ourselves to others and back to us again.

Giving is not a debt you owe, but a seed you sow.

What is a seed? It's potential energy. If it receives the right nutrients, it will grow and help foster an ecosystem that begets and sustains even more growth. So when you give your money, you're truly planting seeds.

If you plant a seed of corn, you will harvest

over 170 kernels in return. You reap what you sow. If you plant corn, you won't harvest tomatoes. It's the same with giving. One of the questions I often hear is "I really don't have that much money now. Can I just give my time?"

Well, if you give or plant seeds of *time*, don't expect to harvest money.

Building and sharing affluence will help create a psychology of wealth and abundance from within. It's not necessarily the amount that you give, but rather the ingrained discipline of giving each week that makes the true difference.

If you fail give from your abundance, two things can happen. First, you'll fail to achieve the maximum level of success for which you're destined. Second, you'll likely develop a tendency to hoard money and become obsessed with spending more on yourself.

I once heard a story of how a wealthy man put $1000 in the collection plate at church. One usher said to another, "He had better give. He's got it." And the other usher replied, "I wonder if he's got it because he gives it?"

Now that's the mindset we're going for! And if you have it, it changes everything. If you resist giving, you resist receiving and vice versa. Each is a function of the other. If you neither give nor receive, then you can only take.

Many who have attained a comfortable level of affluence, myself included, have a more difficult time receiving than they do giving—especially from someone who they perceive has less to give.

I used to see a patient named Ruth. She was a little old hunchbacked lady who came in to see me almost every week. And though she never got better, she did always find some relief. Ruth was also a widower whose husband had been a minister. She had very limited income. But the week before one of her visits, she overheard someone wish me a happy anniversary.

When her next visit rolled around, she got off the table, handed me an anniversary card, and excitedly told me to open it. When I opened it, a crumpled five dollar bill fell to the floor. I looked at it, picked it up, and made eye contact with her. I began to mouth the words, "Thank you, but I can't accept this."

After all, from a functional point of view, her money wouldn't change my life at all. I don't want that to sound insensitive or unappreciative, just realistic. But when I saw her face begin to fall as soon as I said "I can't", I changed my language immediately.

I corrected myself and said, "I can't believe you've given me such a generous gift. Of all the patients I've seen in the last week who knew it was my anniversary, you are the only one who has gone as far as to bring me a card—let alone a present. Thank you!"

Ruth lit up like a Christmas tree. She stood taller and smiled proudly. She embodied the adage of "better to give than receive".

Stories like this are very powerful to me. They

demonstrate how we struggle to give if we can't receive. Even something as simple as receiving an anniversary card and the five dollar gift it included was a very memorable and humbling lesson for me.

But what Ruth's story best illustrates is that regardless of your level of affluence, giving is a great joy! So if you've never made a consistent effort to give before, where should you begin?

Your church is a great place to start. Your community, your profession, or alma matter as well.

Your local food pantry, the Special Olympics, the car in the drive-thru behind you. The places to give are virtually unlimited.

If I'm having a bad day or being challenged in my life, I've given money to the first person I met on the street. Believe me, this has prompted some interesting family discussions regarding money, stewardship and responsibility. The first time my wife saw me give a less fortunate fellow some cash, she questioned my sanity. She said he was probably headed to the nearest liquor store with this newfound cash. The money would have been better off staying in my wallet than fueling his problems.

My response then, as it is today, parallels the foundational principle that money is a form of energy. I'd done my part by sharing wealth and what that man did with it was his responsibility. Once the money left my hands, it was no longer "mine" and I gave up my right to tell it how to behave.

Be careful with your giving and ensure that you don't develop the habit of giving with strings attached. Because then, it is no longer a gift but a transaction. "I'll give you this if you agree to do that". Or in the case of that man, "if you agree *not* to do that".

It doesn't matter if it's $100,000 or the five dollars that I came very close to hurting Ruth's feelings over. You must respect the energy that money possesses. Look at your kids on Christmas Day. Do you get more excitement when watching them open a gift from you, or when you open your gifts from them?

It's giving that makes it easy to receive. It is two parts of one beautiful function directly linked to the other. By creating a Giving Account, you are not only establishing the habit of giving. You are also opening yourself up to the prospect of receiving. You are communicating to the universe (and yourself) that you are an open portal for the energy of money and abundance to flow in your life.

CHAPTER QUESTIONS

1. What cause(s) are you passionate about?

2. What would financially supporting it mean to you?

3. How much can you start giving?

This money is meant to be spent and act as a reward for your accomplishments along your journey to financial freedom.

CHAPTER 10
Fun Account

You've made it to the end! Trust me, this account won't disappoint. It's the easy one!

Consider the Fun Account your debt-reduction stress release valve. As you eliminate debt and accumulate wealth, you need to have some fun along the way. If you simply work, pay debts, and deposit into savings, odds are you'll fall off the bandwagon. Fun will help balance the tremendous effort and disciplined choices you're making in every other area.

So here's a thought. The Fun Account is your authorized "stupid money".

As my wife and I went through the initial debt-reduction strategy years ago, we did so with laser-beam focus. We paid off all of our debt, including our house, in about twenty-four months.

We were pleased to finally be debt-free after two years of intense financial belt-tightening. But we were in a bit of a relational funk and stressed out from the process. As we reflected back on this period, we coined the term "Debt-Reduction Stress."

Everything we did and thought about revolved around getting out of debt. And we did, but at the cost of being unbalanced. We didn't have any debt, but we also had no money and very little fun along the way. Honestly, we would have been hard-pressed to continue with that lifestyle much longer.

The idea of a Fun Account was added to the 7 Accounts System at the same time I decided the Debt-Reduction Account should not contain all discretionary income. While the original approach will seriously ramp up your velocity toward a debt-free life, it will also generate debt-reduction stress in your relationships. You can be a "financial zero" in a short period of time like we were, but also without assets and with little fun along the way.

While the time to reduce debt is longer in today's system, you will have accumulated funds and enjoyed the journey.

RENT THE EXPERIENCE

Several years ago, my business partners, my wife, and myself went on a trip to Ireland. We stayed in the stunning Waterford Castle—a 16th century, seventeen room castle that rests on a private island along the Suir River. It was unbelievable.

We explored the castle one evening, wandering form room to room until we found ourselves in an impressive study. We were so caught up in the experience that we didn't notice anyone else in the room until a man cleared his throat. It turned out to be the owner sitting at his desk and we had wondered into his personal study!

Graciously, he offered us a glass of port or scotch and we enjoyed a cocktail with him. As we talked, it came up that the castle was actually for sale, albeit for an astronomic price. Obviously, buying a 16th century castle on a private island in Ireland is unrealistic.

But, you know what isn't? Renting the experience!

Renting an incredible experience instead of buying one is a prime way to make the most of your Fun Account. Because the more you own, the more you preclude yourself from other experiences. For instance, if we'd somehow managed to purchase that castle, guess what we'd be doing every summer? Going to our Irish castle. Now, that wouldn't be the worst thing in the world. But we'd miss out on so much more that we'd like to explore because we'd have obligated ourselves to this one experience.

On another outing, we rented a five-bedroom catamaran and sailed the British Virgin Islands. It was the single best trip we've ever been on. Our captain was a scuba diving instructor and his girlfriend was a gourmet chef. It was the perfect vacation.

So naturally we thought, "We should buy a boat!" But

guess what? It's been well over twenty years now and we still haven't gone back. Just like that castle in Ireland, it was a wonderful experience. But not one that we wanted to repeat over and over.

However, it's a trade-off. We owned a lake cabin for twenty years because we all loved it. Did my family go to Disney World? Once. As a family, we were spending too much time at the cabin.

I'm not saying you should never own anything. You simply need to understand that no matter what you buy, it's not about the thing itself. It's about the experience it offers. For us, the cabin offered times that, as a family, we wanted to enjoy again and again. Remember, you can have anything you want. You just can't have everything.

I don't need to own a catamaran the best money can buy when we want to sail across the Caribbean. I don't need to own a castle in Europe to enjoy an incredible time. Renting your experiences versus owning them is one of the hallmarks between the affluent and the rich. Renting can replicate the experience without the hassles, maintenance, and expense of ownership. Enjoy the experience!

A FEW WORDS OF CAUTION

Some of our clients that have used the 7 Accounts System have had issues with the Fun Account because they thought it was just their personal fun money. They would buy new golf clubs, skis, mountain bikes, and any other toys they wanted. But everything was for themselves. However, this money is to be spent on both you and your family.

It's also designed so that the money would be spent like its namesake. It should be fun! These funds shouldn't be spent frivolously but certainly not as "seriously" as the money in your other accounts. It's neither money that should be deducted from your House Account nor funds to be used for an extra mortgage payment. It is truly for a reward or something fun for you and your family.

Again, this may seem counterintuitive because it is. Disciplining yourself to change your behavior and your destiny is a challenge. But if you follow this plan and see periodic rewards along the way, then staying the course is much easier and more fun.

Save for it and then spend it. This is not money to be saved long-term. It's meant to be spent and act as a reward for your incremental accomplishments along your journey to financial freedom.

Pay off a debt? Take your spouse out for a nice dinner to celebrate! Child's birthday? Do something out of the ordinary! When your Fun Account is properly funded, you can read the menu from left to right for a change.

There are truly no limits on what your Fun Account money can be spent on. Vacations, family activities, a shopping spree— the sky's the limit! The caveat is you only get to spend as much as you have saved and only from this account.

Remember, we are not "mingling" funds. If you have money in the Tax Account, that money has already been "spent" and is not available to contribute to the Fun Account. No inter-account borrowing is allowed!

When you use your Fun Account appropriately, you and your family's overall quality of life will continue to improve while still making great financial strides forward.

CHAPTER QUESTIONS

1. What's at the top of your fun list?

2. What experiences can you rent instead of purchase?

3. How can you make your fun account available to your family?

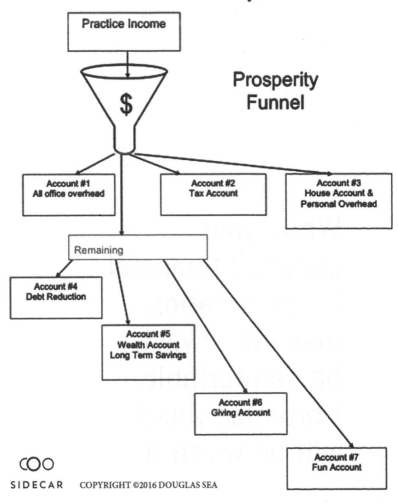

Seven Accounts System

Practice Income

Prosperity Funnel

$

Account #1
All office overhead

Account #2
Tax Account

Account #3
House Account &
Personal Overhead

Remaining

Account #4
Debt Reduction

Account #5
Wealth Account
Long Term Savings

Account #6
Giving Account

Account #7
Fun Account

While your
personal financial
transformation
may not always
be comfortable,
I promise you it
will be worth it.

CONCLUSION
Bringing It All Together

There are three key relationships that govern us all. The relationship we have with ourselves, with others, and with money. All of the key relationships are intricately related and can be self-perpetuating. It has been said that if you love what you do, you never go to work again. While this is a catchy platitude, the real world often crafts a different reality. I have found there is no "Job Nirvana". I truly loved my job of being a chiropractor. Helping people regain their health and hope was incredibly fulfilling to me. But, like any career, there were parts that I found routine, monotonous, and stressful.

My willingness to change my "self-talk", my beliefs, and take massive action changed my professional success path. History, it has been said, repeats itself. I believe history or "your story" is a predictor of the future, not a mandate. If you like the path you are on, continue to think the same thoughts, and take the same actions, you will continue to get more of what you have got. If you do not like your current direction, begin thinking differently and this will cause you to act differently. Action trumps everything. Changing your self-view will change how you view yourself as well as others. It starts here. Discipline your self-talk.

The success I've enjoyed in my career has blessed me in all my key relationships. The relationships are aligned and related. By embodying the principles outlined in *Seven*, I disciplined my relationship with and developed a tremendous amount of respect for the tool we call money. This financial discipline instilled in me the ability to be a good steward of wealth.

Seven's systems, rules of engagement, and understanding of affluence are designed to help you create a life beyond what you may have ever dreamt possible. I am fully aware of *Seven's* success in my life and am confident you too can have a life truly worth living.

Will it be work? Absolutely!

Will it require discipline? For sure!

Will it be uncomfortable? Yes! Here is the reality. You will be uncomfortable either way. What I mean is there is always a tradeoff.

Being an over-weight couch potato, having elevated blood pressure, or living with low energy entertains a certain level of discomfort in all aspects of a person's life. While someone who eats well, exercises, and is mentally healthy experiences discomfort too. It isn't always fun going to the gym before breakfast. The difference is not the level of discomfort. It's the reward at the end. So while your personal financial transformation may not always be comfortable, I promise you it will be worth it.

I would love to hear about your success as you follow the principles taught in *Seven*. Please feel free to email me at drsea@sidecaredge.com to share your story and ask for advice amidst any challenges you face.

Be sure to visit www.sidecaredge.com/sidecar-services/seven to download all of the resources discussed in this book, as well as a bonus whitepaper, *Critical Thinking vs. Conventional Wisdom*, where I discuss even more uncommon principles of affluence.